Mandalas Reflections From Inner Space

Jan West

2nd edition. Updated and expanded, 2021

AuthorHouse™
1663 Liberty Drive
Bloomington, IN 47403
www.authorhouse.com
Phone: 833-262-8899

This book is printed on acid-free paper.

ISBN: 978-1-4772-9047-7 (sc)
ISBN: 978-1-4772-9048-4 (e)

Library of Congress Control Number: 2012921742

Print information available on the last page.

Published by AuthorHouse 11/08/2021

author HOUSE®

This book is dedicated to my cubs, Luke, Whitney, Gabriel and Colleen, and to my grandchildren Zachary, Tyler and Isabelle. I love you to infinity and beyond. To my parents, John and Patricia Hungerford, words fail me. Thank you for your endless love and support. You filled all of our lives with riches beyond count and made everything so much fun. To my prolific and brilliant sister, Jill Hungerford, thank you. Thank you for all you do for all of us. Never stop creating Jill, you are amazing.

To my mentors Susan and William Walsh, you have become my teachers, my friends, my family, my task masters, but mostly, my guiding light. Thank you for sharing your genius and love with me. To my family and friends, who have stood by me and believed in me, I thank you with all my heart. You have made my journey beautiful, and have filled my life with love and meaning.

Jan West

Dear Reader,

Welcome to my wonderful world of circles, spheres and mandalas. This book is created from an artist and a seekers vantage. I invite the viewer to interpret my work in any way that has personal meaning. I don't create from a religious or didactic platform. I have no interest in professing an ideology or theology. I offer both my art and my musings symbolically and not literally.

A long time ago, I became a lover of stories and mythology and a student of indigenous cultures, beliefs and practices. I also became an unschooled lover of quantum physics and other frontier sciences. Even though my brain couldn't grasp the full mechanics of the science, I have absorbed some of the concepts, which I apply to my artwork. I have been a loner on my creative path and never a joiner of groups. I think my introverted nature, my homogenized heritage, and my resistance to following, has kept my mind open to new ideas.

Today's technology offers a powerful metaphor for working with the invisible realms. In the modern world, most of us use invisible forces daily. Cell phones, webs, lasers, etc… are examples of common devices that do things for us. They operate on invisible frequencies and systems that are unfathomable to most of us. The technological era provides a powerful template for understanding our connection to the invisible domains. A triad made up of our physical, mental and energetic bodies and our ability to enter into relationship with these principles, is central to the new paradigm of reality.

The times they are a changing. People are becoming more and more familiar with energetics and invisible forces. The magnitude of the shift of consciousness, that is occurring within the general population is mythic in proportion. We are moving into a unique era, where the foundation is shifting from one based on a physical reality to an energetic one. Mandalas can teach us how to grow and evolve along with the changes that are occurring throughout our world. I believe the new frontier is that of the interior. It is the journey inward that explores and exposes new horizons.

My work is inspired by a pure love of the creative process. Any aspirations I have, are to inspire others to stand in the center of their own power. I think all great poetry, literature, music, mythology and art, inspires the observer to move towards their own personal truth. My hope would be, that someone might read my words or look at my art and be inspired with a brand new idea, or a call to creativity, or a moment of joy. It is with that intention that I present *Mandalas: Reflections From Inner Space.* Thank you for your time. Please enjoy.

Contents:

Mandalas
Reflections From Inner Space

Outer Space. Inner Space. Possibilities of Space.

Mine, Yours, Ours; Sacred Space.

In the metaphor of our existence,

May we all see the light of Infinite Space.

Introduction

Mandalas can help change your reality with a touch of mystery and a hint of magic!

Mandalas are stories depicted symbolically and energetically in a circle. They can be used as a healing tool or a pathway into the divine or can simply be enjoyed as art. They are found everywhere, both in nature and in man-made creations. The contemplation of a mandala is meant to bring inner peace and a feeling that life has once again found its meaning and order.

Mandalas are a symbolic representation of universal balance and love and can be used to assist a seeker in his or her search for wholeness and self-actualization. They are a visual and often beautiful representation of the circle of life. They are designed to support the seeker's inward journey. Mandalas can be used to bring the observer's mind, body, and soul into alignment with his or her own personal truth.

Meditating on a mandala provides a way for a practitioner to enter a sacred space. The space is internal and is free of external noise and influence. It is a place of non-doing where we open to the whispers of the universe. It is here that we experience bliss. One might feel a reunion with spirit or an overwhelming sense of love and well-being. Some find answers to questions when they step into their center. Others are guided toward paradigm shifts in their thinking. Some are inspired creatively or with a new and original idea. Mandalas can be used as a gateway into your place of peace and centeredness. They are portals into a sanctuary where we find balance, truth, love, and empowerment. Mandalas gently lead us inward.

A characteristic of good art is that it has more than one layer. It shifts and grows with the viewer or the listener and it offers a fresh experience over time. Mandalas are transformational tools. By entering into and spending time with a mandala, the viewer is afforded an opportunity to change. There is a transference of energy and consciousness from the art to the seeker. The mandala becomes the transmitter and connector, and the viewer becomes the receptor and the translator. The dance between tool and individual can be transformative. The newly inspired, then can go back out into the world, as a fully charged and balanced participant in the circle of life.

West uses art to explore mystery. Her work explores the interconnectedness of all. Jan hopes that the stories in her mandalas will speak to you. All of the mandalas presented in this book are hand-painted or created with a combination of paint and photography by Jan West.

Historical Reference

A mandala, medicine wheel, magic circle, orb, labyrinth, sphere, or any other variation of a sacred circle refers to the expression of the psyche and in particular of self, in its most perfect and whole state of being. Mandalas are an example of an archetypal form, which means that they have been found throughout time, from all parts of the globe, and in dramatically different cultures.

The mandala was psychiatrist Carl Jung's favorite psychological tool. He often had his patients create mandalas as part of their therapeutic process. Renowned teacher Joseph Campbell taught that mandalas are tools for personal meditation, healing, and self-realization. He said "the mandala will coordinate your circle within the universal circle and be instrumental in helping you to follow your bliss."

For Tibetan Buddhists, mandalas are thought to be the "architecture for enlightenment." For the Hindus, they are "bridges into the metaphysical realm." Native Americans use mandalas (medicine wheels or structured sand paintings) to bring a sick person back into harmony with himself and with the cosmos, and thereby to restore health. In Eastern civilizations, mandala pictures are used to consolidate the inner being or to enable one to plunge into a deep meditation. In the metaphysical community, mandalas are energy-retention devices that make entry into the intuitive realms more accessible.

The stories in the mandalas are about our connection to each other, to mystery, and to the archetypal realm. Meditate on a mandala and listen to the stories in your heart, as they are whispered to you by your inner knowing.

I hope the stories in my mandalas will speak to you. We each have a unique vision. I invite you to celebrate yours and to vigorously participate in the dance of the universe.

Art As Metaphor

In addition to being appreciated as art, and for their innate beauty, mandalas can be used as a meditation tool that will work with you precisely where you are in your present-day life. The nature of a symbolic and energetic healing tool is that it is not static. It is ever changing. The symbols painted into the mandala will shift and grow with you over time, if you invite them to. Symbolic art works both intellectually and intuitively. It can help transform dreams, intentions, thoughts, and prayers into physical reality.

Each symbol has a vibration and a frequency that can jump off the printed page to work with your specific needs at a given moment. Vibrational healing tools are never static, which is another way of saying that they are energetic by nature. They are able to shift and to resonate with what you need at any given moment.

Thoughts and emotions have an energy of their own. Their vibrations shift and change from moment to moment. Thoughts and emotions have their own frequencies and pathways. They are dynamic. The symbols in the mandalas are receptors for your thoughts, prayers and intentions. When you enter into a relationship with them, they can serve as a map, that will guide you toward your most powerful self.

Deep realization can lead to profound transformation. When a veil lifts and we experience a paradox shift in our perception of reality, we raise our vibration. In those moments, we transcend the mundane. We are, in those times, capable of not only change but also the evolution of our soul. True transformation and change occurs when our mind, body, and soul are in perfect sync.

We live in a technological era. Every day, we use the internet, smart phones, and other mind-blowing inventions. Our familiarity with technology helps us bridge the gap between the world of brick and mortar and that of the intangible, consciousness dimensions. Not too long ago, these concepts of invisible forces were the fodder of fairytales. Today, in America, most of us use technology regularly. The devices function beyond most of our actual understanding. We just expect them to work. We don't see the process, but we rely heavily upon the expected outcome.

It isn't a giant leap to think of ourselves in a similar manner. We are fundamentally operating from an invisible power source. In many ways, advancements in technology make the world of consciousness more accessible and more immediate. Thought creates matter. Energy follows awareness. Thoughts matter. The invisible realms were once only accessed by mystics and sages. Now many are starting to believe that *they* have access to the 'world of the mystery' as well.

Another metaphor that exemplifies the dynamics of working with a mandala and the energetic process of manifesting an intention, is that of planting a seed. The metaphor is, that the center is the place with the richest soil and the perfect balance of sun and rain. Our job as gardener, is to step into the center with absolute focus and commitment. When we do so, we step into a perfect balance with our mind, body, spirit, and with universal truth. From this vantage, we see that we are never alone and that we are entirely alone. Paradox abounds in all truth. So be it.

From the center, the place where inspiration lives, you must choose carefully the seed that you are going to plant. From a place of non-judgment and innocence, you are most receptive to inner guidance. Trust yourself as you select the perfect seed to plant. Choose the one that generates the greatest anima, a burning passion within you. Plant the seed carefully and correctly. The seed will have everything it needs to flourish, as do you. After you plant the seed of your dream, you will have to wait for the idea to take root. As the roots begin to form and the plant begins to grow toward the light, you will enter a hustle-and-bustle of work and ideas.

New shoots are tender and fragile, as are young ideas and dreams. Be careful at this time with whom you share your dreams. Choose thoughtfully whom you will invite into your sacred garden at this time. Share your incubation period with only a few trusted people who will support your process. Tend to your seed diligently as it matures. As you nurture your dream from this center of power and wisdom, do so habitually. Give it proper amounts of water, fertilizer, sunlight, and whatever else it may require. There is, however, in this process a time to let go. At some point, one must know that, for the time being, the appropriate action has already been taken. There is a time in this process when we do without doing. We simply hope and trust that the seed will grow to fruition. There is a time for planting and a time for harvesting. For everything, there is a season. The smallest seedling can grow into a mighty oak.

We are born with a full tool kit, with everything we will ever need to fulfill our highest potential. The tricky part is balancing out the ups and downs along the way. Emotional, mental, and physical demands are a constant fact of life. Balancing life's challenges and tragedies with our hopes, dreams and goals is the challenge. None of us can live at the pinnacle. Peak moments are fleeting, but forever ours. Moments of illumination are few and far between, but they guide and encourage us to keep seeking and trying. You can't hit a target without aiming and shooting. This stage of creativity is about showing up and doing the work. The important thing is to always move toward the light. Buddha's last words were, "Do your best." One's best will always be good enough.

My purest moments slip in uninvited. They occur when I am where I need to be, doing what I need to be doing. Perfect moments come most often to me when I am with those I love, or in nature, or when I am creating. You will have your own access ramps and vehicles toward what is most important to you. We are all dynamic beings. We are energetic bundles of consciousness and love. Our connection to personal power and wisdom lives at our center. Right here. Right now. Believe it or not … perfection.

The contemplation of a mandala can help restore balance. If you allow yourself to sit with one and to still your noisy mind, you may find that a new idea might slip in through the back door. A mandala may amplify your mediation, intensify your connection to your creative forces, or reveal opportunities to you, where before there were only questions, fears, and dead ends. Joseph Campbell said it best when he instructed his students to, "Follow your bliss."

I believe *bliss* is the map we are given to follow, to guide us on our journey on this beautiful, fragile planet earth. Life's roads are twisted and challenging. Our guideposts light up or dim, dependent upon the choices we make along the way. Always move toward the option that makes your heart pound and your world seem brighter. It's that simple. It's that difficult. Once again, a paradox.

Circle Stories

The stories in the mandalas are about our connection to each other and to the universal heartbeat. It is this awareness and understanding that generates healing energies. Allow your mind to quiet and your eyes to travel quietly around the colors and symbols. The symbols in the mandalas are energetic and interactive conduits. They can serve as check-in-points on a seekers path and as portals into silence. I invite you to journey deeply into your center and to open to the whispers of the ancients.

Mandalas create powerful energetic vortexes that amplify intuition and receptivity to guidance. Life on earth and in the fourth dimension, can be thought of as a holographic experience. We are dancing between dimensions all the time. The physical world and the worlds made up of energy and consciousness are all connected. Symbolic tools such as mandalas, connect us with the eternal force that creates and drives everything. When we think of ourselves as a whirling, spinning, bundle of frequencies and vibrations, we better understand how powerful thoughts are, and how easily manipulated physical reality can be.

The symbols in the paintings will shift and change to meet you where you are at a given moment. Your relationship with a mandala will change along with your growth process. Your seeking heart, will guide you along your journey and lead you to where you need to be. The communication that develops with the mandala and with the intuitive realms will be unique to you. It will be fueled by your personal dreams, aspirations and purpose.

May your journey be filled with wonder and awe, and may you continue to cultivate your life with grace and beauty. Step into your sacred center and recognize your magnificence.

Jan's Creative Process

When I am about to begin a mandala, either for myself or for another, I allow myself to step out of my daily life and into the realm of the mystical. It is as concrete as changing from a fedora to a cowboy hat. I feel a change in myself at a molecular, cellular level. I get tingly and happy, and I know that I am about to dance with the sublime. The reason I can do this on a dime, is because I am practiced and disciplined. It always comes down to showing up and doing the work.

When I was a mother of young children, I realized quickly that I had to find a way to create my artwork and care for my family at the same time. My cubs are now young adults. All of them learned early on, that when I was painting, I lost track of space and time. We learned that they could say, "Mom, come..." and it could be hours before I came up for air. The arrangement we quickly established, was that if they touched my arm, I put the brush down. My agreement with my creative self was that I was going to have to be able to create from the theater of a busy home life filled with lots of distractions. That was the only way I would be able to do business with the muse. I would encourage others to make the same kind of contracts with their creative source. Figure out what works for you and set clear boundaries. These agreements can be changed as often as needed, but the important thing is consistency. Daily practice is best, but the bottom line is showing up.

If I am creating a mandala as a commission for someone, the first thing I do, is to ask him or her for permission to enter his or her sacred space with my intention, only for the time it takes me to create the mandala. I assure the person that my intentions are good and that I will only work with high integrity, light, and love. Once we agree on that, the fun begins. I ask the person to become a squirrel and to gather, gather, gather photos, magazine clippings, ideas, hopes, dreams, colors, ethnic preferences, and everything that he or she wants to bring into his or her life. I also ask the person to consider what he or she wants to release and what they do not want to bring into their life. We talk until I have a clear intellectual handle on what he or she wants his or her personal mandala to be.

I then take the material back into my cave (my studio) and begin processing my intentions for the mandala. I reflect on my client's wishes both consciously and meditatively. When I paint, I set my thinking cap aside. I let go of conscious thought. I let go of how I think the mandala should turn out. I step into the void and begin to paint.

The base coat of a mandala looks like a bull's-eye that one might use for target practice. It is almost comical how uninspiring the painting looks at this stage of its development. I have come to accept the fact that the painting of the bull's-eye is the most critical stage of the process. If a mandala takes 300 hours to paint, the bull's-eye will take 150 hours. It is not because I don't know how to paint circles. It's because it is the foundation of the painting and my creative and intuitive process. With each brushstroke, I am painting into the base of the mandala intentions, hopes, dreams, and prayers. I am enlivening the painting with an energy of its own. I am breathing life into the mandala with each well-intended stroke.

The fun part is filling in the symbols, codes, and sacred geometries that are built into each mandala. It is the combined energy of the bull's-eye base and the different designs and patterns that make one mandala different from another. Intention plays a big role here. I am using the paint and canvas as a vehicle and as a bridge between the physical and non-physical worlds.

A footnote is that if something is not meant to be in the mandala, I can't paint it. I have come to trust this process and no longer fight it.

It is obvious to me when a mandala is finished. I become still and I feel satisfied and complete. I give thanks and symbolically wrap the painting in a blanket of luminescent light. I also energetically activate the mandala so that it can go out into the world and work its magic.

Using Mandalas for Healing, Direction and Guidance

What to Do When the Road Gets Bumpy.

There are times in life when the only correct action is non action. These times may feel like limbo or even hell. It's easy to think we are trapped in a never ending holding pattern at ground zero, but what we are doing is riding a wave. Often we feel abandoned and lost. We are not. This too, is a part of our process. Trust and hope are lifelines, no matter how insignificant or feckless they may appear to be. In these times, there is work being done under the surface. It is often out of the reaches of our thinking mind.

Sometimes we must retreat to heal. When we step into our sacred center, we step into a sanctuary, a chrysalis of healing. Guidance and assistance are waiting for us when we arrive. The alchemist patiently waits for our arrival so she can begin to work her magic. The big challenge for us, is letting go and opening ourselves to grace.

"All that you are seeking is also seeking you.

If you lie still, sit still, it will find you.

It has been waiting for you a long time."

Clarissa Pinkola Estes

Symbolically, we can look to the life cycle of a butterfly as a map between the internal and the external. A butterflies' life begins as an egg that moves through the larva stage and emerges a caterpillar. When it is ready, the caterpillar will find a special place, to shed its skin and to transform into a chrysalis. The chrysalis is similar to a cocoon. Amazingly, the chrysalis is already formed beneath the skin of a caterpillar. It emerges, as the caterpillar sheds its skin for the last time.

Inside the chrysalis, a magical transformation is taking place. When ready, a fully formed butterfly breaks free and takes flight. Butterflies are beautiful. They live fully in the present moment. They innately know what they were born to do and they do it. At the appropriate time, the adult butterfly lays its eggs, continuing the circle of life. Birth, Life, Death and Rebirth. It is the natural order of things. In this metaphor, the butterfly is one with the *Dance*.

Somewhere along the way, most of us learn that life can be as *"horrible"* as it is *"marvelous"*. The obvious goal of course, is to always move towards *"marvelous"*. Pretty easy to do when times are good. Very difficult, when times are bad. When *"horrible"* raises its angry head, life gets hard. At these times we must move forward, propelled by a blind, unfathomable faith.

We have a choice point here. The best choice, is to gather our strength and fortitude and to become one with the warrior archetype. By standing steadfast, no matter how shaky our legs are, and fighting for what we know is our personal truth, we are choosing not to be a tragic figure. The act of standing alone, is lonely and scary. Sometimes we are guided only by a wobbly hunch. Our assurance, as to the correctness of our path, is often overshadowed by self-doubt and uncertainty. If you know instinctively, that something is wrong, then be mighty and fierce and fight for justice. Don't be afraid to speak the truth, even if your voice shakes. When we follow in the hero's footsteps, we are choosing courage over fear and action over submission.

My advice here, is to just do something. It is almost impossible to generate action from inertia. If you don't know how to start or what to do, then do anything that does not cause harm. Doing the next best thing, is always a good choice. Before a performance at the Metropolitan Opera, when the performers are preparing to go on stage, the artists often say to each other "Into the mouth of the wolf". And so it is with life. Movement creates movement. Your frequencies and vibrations are shifting with your new activity and your intentions are paving the way for you. Hold your course and move forward steadily.

This is still a time of introversion. Ask for help if you need it. At this time, we cannot be tied to outcome. The job is to show up habitually, to do your work the best you can, most of the time, to find joy and an appreciation of beauty, while supporting others in your circles of influence. That's the job. I don't believe failure is a part of that equation. Somehow through all of this, we profoundly know, that we are being guided by wisdom. Progress is often, from our diminished perspective, minuscule. But there comes a day, when we look around and see that we are no longer where we were. Miles have been traveled. A moment of recognition occurs, that *"horrible"* is no longer our constant companion. We begin to feel centered, and more stable and once in a while we catch glimpses of *"marvelous"*!

What is certain, is the constancy of cycles. Winter, Spring, Summer and Autumn. North, East, South and West. Participant, Spectator, Pedestrian and Inspired. Birth, Life, Death and Rebirth. These are the cycles of life. Rebirth is promised, because it is a part of the great axiom of circles. Trust yourself and trust your place in the universe. Journey frequently into your inner space. Gather the rejuvenating tools you need to move forward, and then jump full throttle, back into the day. I hope we all choose to say, a big ecstatic YES to the dance!

10 Suggestions on How to Use Your Mandala

1. Enjoy it as artwork.

Frame and place your mandala in your home or on your meditation altar. Mandalas will help shift the energy of a room and positively affect any space they occupy.

2. Use it for healing for yourself or others.

Place a photograph—of yourself, a friend, or a relative whom you want to channel energy and healing to—on top of or near your mandala. The power vortex of the mandala will aid you at an energetic level and assist you with your healing and spiritual practice. One way it does so is by amplifying the vibration and frequency of your thoughts and prayers. It brings your intention from the consciousness dimension down into a more concrete or physical form. Visualize the outwardly radiating circles that occur when a stone is thrown into water. The process of working with a mandala is similar to that.

3. Use it as meditation tool.

Place the mandala in front of you while meditating. Eyes open or closed? It really doesn't matter! The vibrations of the mandala in conjunction with your intentions will assure your connection with the frequencies of the mandala. Or … slightly close your eyes, just enough to block out most of the environment, and focus on the center of the mandala. Breathe deeply. Let the moment connect with your essence; inspiration, abundance, strength, and healing. All that you want to bring into your life is now accessible. You are safe and surrounded with divine love and light. The portal to your center is open. Your connection with the consciousness realms is charged and activated. Close your eyes and allow the magic circle to guide you into a deep and inspired meditative state. Allow yourself to receive. You do not have to *do* anything. Receive grace. Do without doing.

4. Use it for manifestation.

Write down your desires onto a piece of paper. For example, "I am now manifesting _____ into my life. Thank you for helping me to manifest my dreams, as they lead me toward the fulfillment of my highest purpose here on earth. I ask that this be done swiftly, properly, and with harm to no one." Place the paper between your hands and hold it to your heart. Close your eyes and visualize having what you want to bring into in your life. Fill your mind and heart with gratitude and joy as you visualize your desire manifested. Place the paper with the writing face down on top of the mandala. If you want to, you can place a crystal, a rock, or a special item on top of the paper. Leave it for seven days and let go. Give your intention to the universe in a field of light. So be it.

5. Use it as an energy vortex and gateway.

Set the mandala on a table or on your altar. Select your favorite crystal(s) or stones and clear them under running water or energetically with bright white light. You can use any symbolic object you want. It does not have to be a rock. Place your symbolic tool on the mandala. This will allow the energies of the vortex to collect, hold, amplify, and create your intentions into your physical reality. You may also program the objects with the mandala's powerful energies. Carry the "crystal" with you to hold and attract the energies of the mandala with you at all times.

6. Use to enhance your communication with the dreamtime.

Place the mandala next to your bed, on a wall near your bed, or under the bed. The vibrations, frequencies, and energies of the mandala will work with you and communicate with you as you sleep. You may notice an increase in your dreams and the acuteness of your dream messages. Your ability to remember and to work with your dreams will be magnified.

7. Use to open yourself to the wisdom of the universe.

Do without doing. Mandalas touch us at both a conscious and unconscious level. Allow yourself to absorb the healing vibrations of your mandala. Give yourself over to grace. Simply spend time with your mandala, eyes open or closed, and allow it to work its magic with you!

8. Use your Mandala to energize and charge your food and drink with positivity and intention. Place a

mandala near or under your food and drink. A mandala can be laminated or placed in plastic and used as a coaster or as a place mat. The imagery and frequencies and vibrations built into the mandala will work along with your intentions to enhance the healing properties of your food and drink. It is possible that the very molecular structure of your nutrients will shift to benefit your process. Intentions like prayers are powerful. The benefits of using the mandala with your food and drink are enormous.

9. No Limits:

Use your mandala absolutely any way you want to. There are no rights and wrongs and I invite you to use your imagination.

10. Have fun! Laughter is the best medicine.

Mandala Exercise

Choose a mandala that has meaning for you. Pick the image that attracts you right now, or pick a mandala randomly. Clarify in your mind your intention, question, or challenge. It may be something you want to manifest, better understand, heal, or honor. Use the mandala in a focused meditation for a short period of time, a day, or a week, or as long as you wish. Guidance will come to you if you invite it into your daily practice.

Visualize your mind, body, and soul being illuminated. See all your energy flowing freely throughout your body. See yourself as flexible, strong, healthy, and happy. Start your practice with one minute of meditation with your mandala's center as the focus. Allow your thoughts and distractions to drift casually in one ear and out the other. Let them go and return to center. Entering of a state of silence allows your intentions to align with you perfectly. When you are finished, seal your energy field off with a circle of white light, and go on about your day with gratitude and joy.

How to Use Your Mandala As a Healing Tool

The following are some specific ways that mandalas can be used for healing and meditation. I encourage you to be creative and to come up with other uses that will be well suited to your own life.

When starting a meditative practice, always intend that your actions be directed toward light and goodness, with harm to no one. Visualize a luminescent sphere that is protected with goodness and grace, as you enter stillness. Clear your mind of noisy, intentional thinking. By approaching the mandala in a receptive state, that is, in silence, you are creating a clear channel. Feel how you are energetically connecting with the symbols and energies built into the mandala. Everyone has intuition. Practice to access, harness, and use yours. The healing vibrations of the images on the mandalas can be transmitted to you and through you. You will receive answers. Trust what you receive.

There is a strong link between our emotions, physical bodies, and spirits. When the vibration of a certain part of the body is disturbed, it negatively affects the whole. Visualize yourself in perfect balance. While working with the mandalas, remember that you are filled with possibility. You are exactly where you are supposed to be on your journey. Warts and all, life is a process of unveiling and growth. Trust your process. Trust yourself. Launch yourself from the mandala's fulcrum into silence. Your vantage point from the center is illuminated with potential. The messages and insights you gain through these ancient and archetypal images may amaze you with their relevance to your life.

Trust yourself and your intuition. You know more than you think you do.

Suggestions on How to Use Your Mandala Book As an Oracle

Choose a mandala to work with for a period of time. Selecting a single mandala, either with conscious intention or randomly, is the simplest and often most effective use of the mandala book as an oracle. Anytime you need an overview of a situation in a moment of crisis, or when you lack sufficient information to decide what constitutes right action, spend some time with the mandala of your choice. Allow yourself to be receptive to guidance.

Single mandala draw: Select a mandala that attracts you at this moment. You can do so with your eyes open, with a pendulum, by randomly opening the book to a page, or through any other way that works for you. The mandala will help you focus more clearly on your issue and provide you with a fresh perspective. Work with this mandala until your understanding of the issue shifts or until your question is answered.

Drawing a mandala a day: This is an ideal way to work with the powers and symbols of the mandalas effortlessly. Trust whatever ideas slip in at this time.

Three Mandala "Spread": When a situation arises that calls for a more in-depth consideration, the Three Mandala "Spread" can be most helpful. The first mandala you select stands for the overview of the situation. The second mandala you choose, either randomly or specifically, stands for the challenge at hand at the present time. The third mandala selected stands for the immediate course of action required. With an issue clearly in mind, select the mandalas you will be working with for this issue. The words written about the mandala are meant to be a guideline for you to focus your thoughts on. If you want to add a fourth mandala, you can. The fourth card is a projection of the future and the actions required, to assist you.

As you reflect on the symbols and codes built into the mandala, let your mind empty and open to inspiration.

Remember, symbolic healing is rarely literal. Think metaphorically when you receive messages and guidance. Your interpretations and insights will shift and change over time. The healing and inspiration received will mirror your personal transformation and growth.

Jan West

View from the Mountaintop Mandala

Cerro Pedernal, New Mexico

From birth to death, we each embark on a journey. The circle of life has many hills and valleys. Courage comes when we are weak and afraid and we find it within ourselves to choose the brave and correct action. John Wayne said, "It's not courage, if you ain't scared." The hero's journey is all about the choices we make, with and without the support of others, and what we bring back with us after the quest. It's about our soul's evolution.

Life is filled with perfect moments and it is our responsibility to recognize these gifts in our daily life. Often we walk right by beauty without even giving it a glance. I have said with tongue in cheek that if I were god, I would be so sad, because "I gave everyone everything. It's all right there for the taking, and yet so many suffer."

All of us have experienced moments of fulfillment. Times when we have accomplished a goal or have experienced true love or pure joy. These pinnacle moments are when we are centered majestically at the top of our "mountain." Some perfect moments are earned and some come unexpectedly like the appearance of a hummingbird. We can carry these moments with us all the rest of our days.

Use this mandala to place yourself squarely into the center of a time when you felt fabulous. Plant the feeling of you standing triumphantly at the top of your mountain firmly into your core. Use those feelings as energy bursts, as power vortexes, as bliss deposits in your feel-good bank account. With visualization, you can build empowering moments into your muscle memory and into your DNA. You can use these energy deposits as often as you like. They never expire; you can only add to them. They can be used for comfort, motivation, or in any way you require to feel whole.

Perfect Moments Are Forever Gifts.

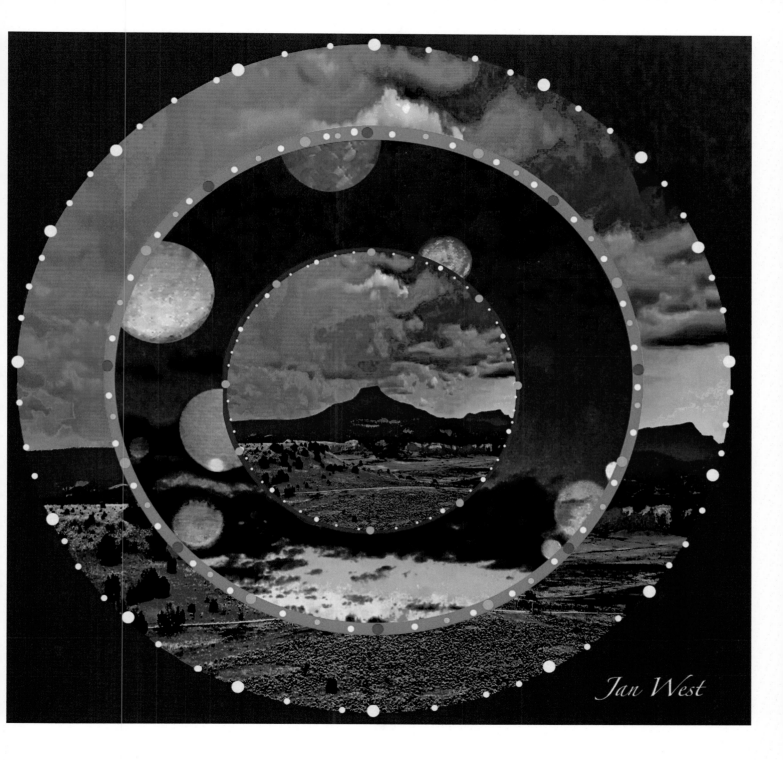

Jan West

Manifesting Dreams Mandala

This healing tool will help transform you and your environment by transmitting positive vibrations that are a part of the force that holds everything together. Our thoughts are mighty. When our perceptions shift, our reality shifts.

Transformation occurs when the mind, body, and soul are in sync. When our actions line up with our intentions, we actually change at a deep core level. Our frequencies are raised and we vibrate more powerfully. Thoughts matter. Energy follows awareness.

Negativity and fear all live down in the lowest frequencies of existence. When people live badly, when they make choices that cause harm, they are functioning at a low vibration. The earth is a classroom. This is a school down here, and we all come to learn lessons that will hopefully help our soul to grow. The process is often painful. We have all been "bad" and we have all been "good."

Our experiences lead to realizations. Realizations lead to growth. Growth leads to transformation. Transformation is growth and change.

When we make good choices that are guided by compassion, kindness, empathy, joy, laughter, and love, we are raising our vibrations. We are raising our frequencies and we are helping our soul to gather strength. I believe this is the human journey. We come down to here to get dirty in the earth, to laugh, to love, and to cry. The process is rarely pretty and often painful, but it's needed for the soul to grow.

If you are working with the Manifesting Dreams Mandala, then it's time for you to leap. You have done your preparation. You are ready and able. It's time to jump into the moment. It's time to say an enthusiastic, "Hell ya!" to your life.

Whatever the appropriate action is, the time is NOW. If you don't take that leap, nothing new will happen and your life force will not grow. Do it. Become a participant, better yet a leader. Your contributions are needed now. We survive together. Keep moving towards light and goodness. Click your heels twice, and realize that the rainbow illuminates all, the pot of gold is within, and with another click of the heels, we are home. Now LEAP.

Jan West

Portal to Your Center Mandala

Daily practice with a mandala will teach you how to access, harness, and use intuitive insights as guidance in your daily life. Transform your daily life into an extraordinary one by stepping frequently into your place of power.

As you view these images, I invite you to put the concerns of everyday life behind you, as well as your duties, obligations, schedules, aspirations, and goals. Allow your gaze to move gently around the periphery and into the center of the image. The center is the inner sanctum and it is the window to the infinite. Allow yourself to step out of your ordinary perceptions and into the realm of the extraordinary. Empty your mind. Let your thoughts drift in and out, in and out, without attachment.

Welcome the silence. Allow yourself to enter the stillness. From your center, the portal of the mandala will open up and invite you in. New experiences may open up to you. Perhaps you will experience a new perception that had been previously hidden from sight.

Welcome a brand new idea into your life!

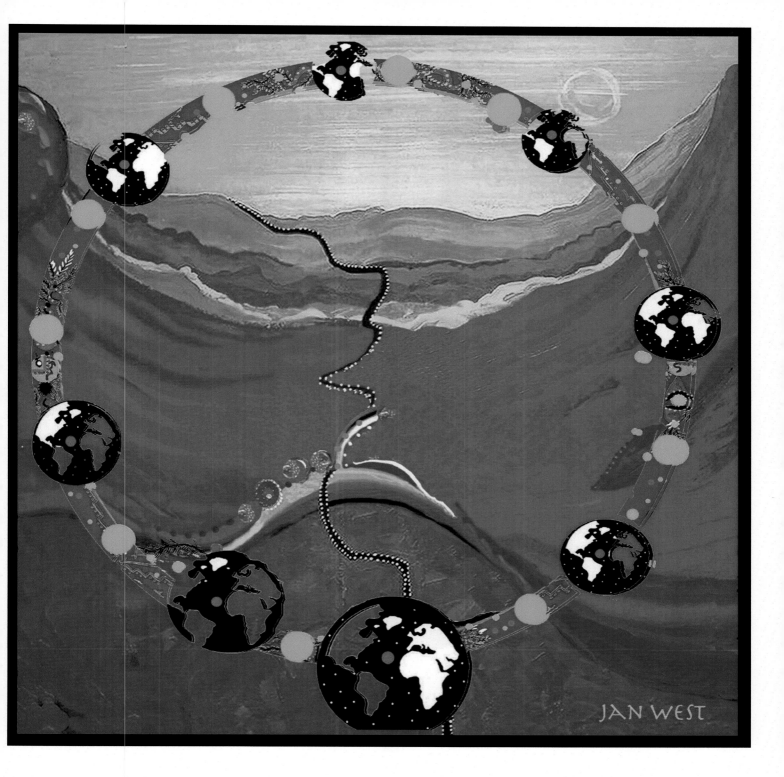

Healed Heart Mandala

Mandalas provide an important map for our wholeness and transformation, both personally and globally. Mandalas invite us into a world that is only limited by our own imagination.

If you can imagine it, then it is real.

As you look at this painting, allow yourself to let go of your rational mind and to slip into the world of uncertainty, mystery, and imagination.

Energetic transformation is the new frontier.

Magic is everywhere. Artists and mystics have depicted these invisible forces throughout the ages. Now, they are accessible to all who open their hearts to love.

Jan West

Sun, Moon and Stars Mandala

Life is precious and far too short

To spend it worrying

What other people think about you.

Laugh, love, and be true to yourself.

Aim for the stars.

Embrace your own magnificence.

It is then, that the heavens open up to you, and support your journey.

Be Bold. Be Mighty. Dream, create, and hold fast to your vision.

Climb high, climb far.

Your goal the sky,

Your aim the stars.

Jan West

Do Your Best
Buddha's Last Words

Passage into Mystery Mandala

This mandala is designed specifically to help you consciously generate abundance in your mind, heart, and world. Feeling abundant and grateful is the first step toward creating it. Use this mandala to attract greater levels of abundance, prosperity, and joy in your life!

"I begin with an idea, and then it becomes something else."

Pablo Picasso

Thought creates matter. Energy follows awareness.

Thoughts matter.

The center is, of course, a symbolic representation of our power center. Invite the realm of the divine into your heart, mind, body, and soul. In this way, you can symbolically step into your divine center. If you can imagine it, then it is real. When we combine our thoughts with intention and hard work, we can change our present-day reality and build our dreams with mortar and stone.

Art is not meant to be created in stolen moments, nor at the end of a long day's work. The creation of art, the process of manifestation, requires energy, effort, focus and anima. Artists bring into physical form the musings of the 'gods', by creating the architecture, the maps, and the information pathways required to move civilization forward.

Art, mythology, storytelling, and all forms of creative efforts, are required for the survival and prosperity of life on earth. They bring in the stories and symbols of new possibility, new quests, new metaphors and new heroes, that we so badly need in these perilous times.

Speak Up
Even If Your
Voice Shakes.

Justice for all.

Practice courage.

Vive la   Resistanc

Speak Up
Even If Your
Voice Shakes.

Speak Up
Even If Your
Voice Shakes.

Speak Up
Even If Your
Voice Shakes.

Art in this context, both its creation and its contemplation, is a vehicle for discovering our own full potential: our divine within. Art is capable of transporting us from the world of the mundane into the world of the mystical.

"Everyone creates realities based on their own personal beliefs. These beliefs are so powerful that they can create [expansive or entrapping] realities over and over."

Kuan Yin

Shaman's Act of Power Mandala

The bold and brightly colored symbols in the *Shaman's Act of Power Mandala* enliven it with the magic and traditions of indigenous people from around the globe. The symbols transcend time and space and will assist you in activating a vortex of vitality and strength from deep within you.

This tool helps amplify mental, emotional, and physical clarity. Use this mandala as a portal into the consciousness realms, and then open yourself to receiving the limitless gifts of the universe.

It is most important to know what your goal is. Have a very clear target, for which you can aim. Allow your time with this mandala to be focused on clarifying what it is you want to manifest in your life. You can have the world's most sophisticated bow and arrow. You can be a world-class marksman. But without a clear target, your chances of success are almost nil.

With the proper equipment, practice, skill, and a clear target, the sky is the limit.

There are no limits.

Jan West

Secrets of the Masters Mandala

The ancient symbolism found in this mandala can activate intuitive wisdom. Meditation on this mandala invokes an intuitive connection to the archetypal realms and can serve as a portal or gateway into the teachings of the ancient mystery schools.

The symbols in this mandala are not only metaphoric but also powerful energy vortexes that can work with you, if you invite them into your world.

Use your light-filled intentions as a key to the ancient gateways of the Egyptian masters.

"Follow your bliss."

Joseph Campbell

Jan West

Activating Intuition with Merkaba Mandala

Inter-Dimensional Communication

Through focused intent, we can activate an energy field, which is known as merkaba, around the human body. Once activated, it is capable of carrying our consciousness to higher dimensions. This mandala is a powerful portal into the mystery realms. It assists in clearing the pathways between dimensions.

For most of us, this portal has been tightly sealed for most of our lives. Activate this mandala when working with dimensions of time and space, such as clearing old physical and emotional pain, energy patterns, and karma. The merkaba is a whirling, swirling geometric portal. It is made up of energy and consciousness.

Allow this mandala to transport you into a newly energized state of being.

Expect big changes.

Awaken and get ready!

"What is now proved was only once imagined."

William Blake

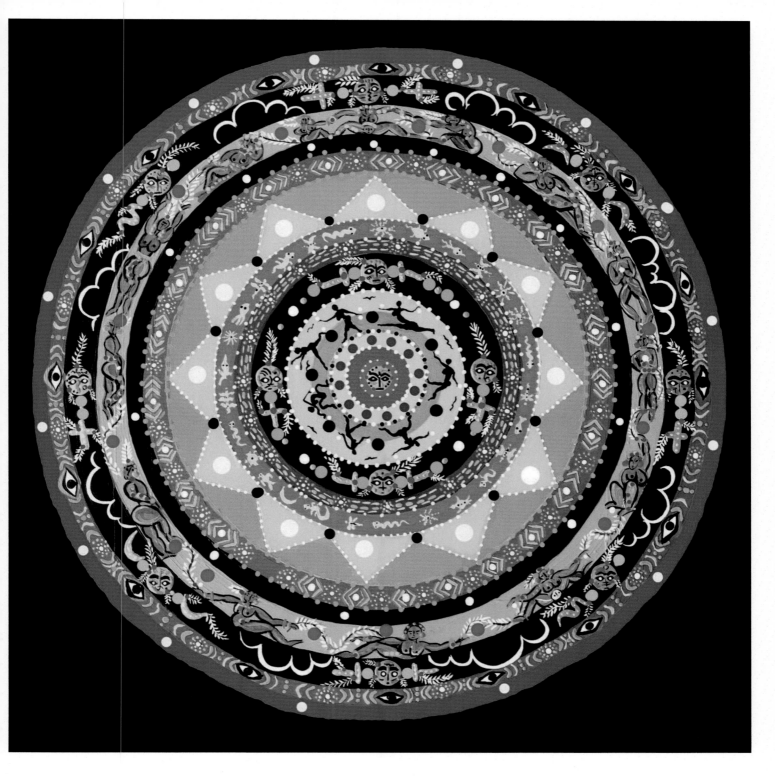

Kundalini Play Mandala

Creativity Lives Within Us All

Like the Kundalini Lizards playing in a circle of plenty, this mandala offers blessings for balance, peace, joy, and creativity. We are hardwired for bliss. All you have to do, is to tap into your own body's unlimited natural capacity for living in joy!

Both Beethoven and Mozart were masters at connecting artistic form with inspiration. Both acknowledged that their music was divinely inspired. Both geniuses were good listeners.

Beethoven was one of the first to put his individual stamp on all his music. His unparalleled greatness and his masterpieces, are a celebration of the individualist spirit.

Mozart on the other hand was a wide open channel for angelic orchestrations. He was willing to let the choirs of the angels sing on their own, without any temptation to put his individual stamp on it.

Thank goodness for the music of these two men, but thank Beethoven and Mozart as well, for showing up and doing the work. Both Beethoven and Mozart were familiar with the journey into Inner Space and then back out again, with a treasure chest full of goodies to share with the world.

Be like the Kundalini Lizards playing in this mandala. Play and dance your way in and out and around your sacred wheel. Throw perfection, shoulds and should nots into the trash bin. Let go of expectations. Laugh, love, create and have fun. Follow your passion.

From your passion comes magic!

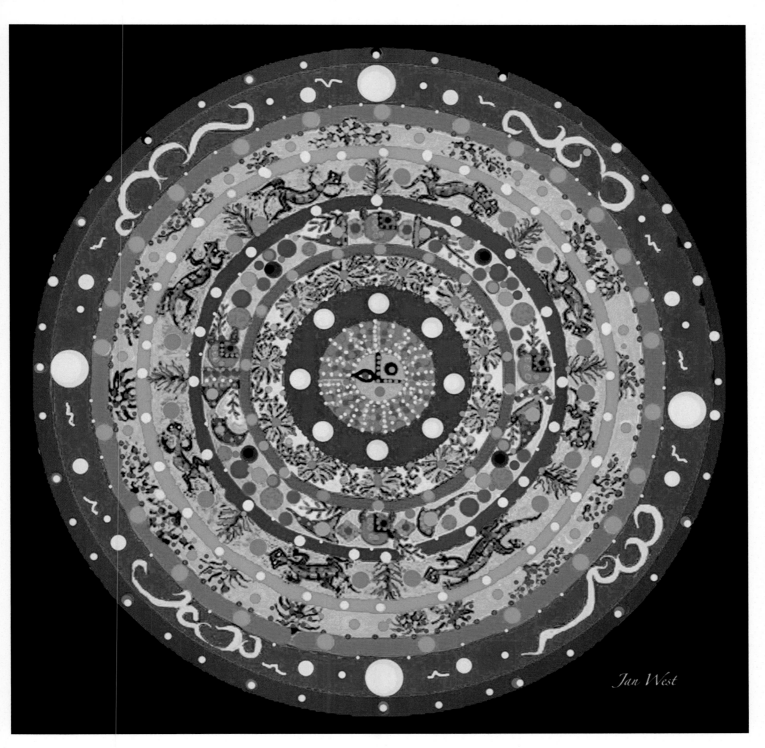

Jan West

Transcending Paradigms Mandala

Ancient Mystery Is Shared With All At The Pow Wow

Meditate, drum, chant, or simply be with this image, to invoke the energies, residing within the mandala. Ask for healing and blessings, for yourself and for the greater good.

A mandala's healing power extends to the whole world.

Benevolent forces are present in this mandala and are available to guide you. Your work with this mandala will always be directed toward your highest purpose. Native American prayers and practices are symbolically programmed into this art.

The fundamental energy of the Transcending Paradigms Mandala is grace. When you open yourself to its influence, you may begin to recognize the signs, symbols, and messages that are placed as guideposts on your life's path.

Mandalas transmit positive energies, frequencies and healing vibrations to the people who view them. Work with the gentle vibrations of this mandala to open your heart to the universal love and wisdom that is accessible to all who seek it.

Open to the heartbeat of the earth.

Receive the blessing of the sacred drum.

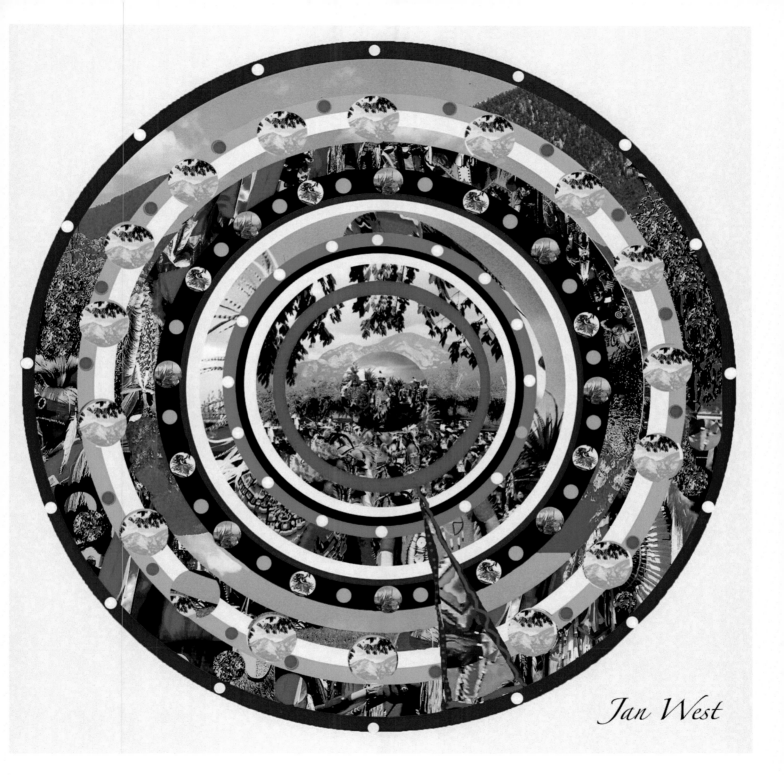

Jan West

Child's Play Mandala

Joyful Union and Healing with Your Inner Child

This mandala with its playful symbols of childlike joy and blissful energy, will help assist you in activating a vortex of vitality. Feel the wind beneath your wings as you sail the seven seas into the magical realms of imagination, creativity, and unbridled potential.

Now you can unlock the force of courage and inner strength within your mind and change your life, by awakening your child within.

Children laugh and play. They cry when they are hurt or sad. They accept what is. They accept comfort and help when needed. Their innocence protects them and guides them. Learn from a child how to view the world with open eyes. Learn from your care of a child, how to care for yourself.

"Life isn't about waiting for the storm to pass.

It's about learning how to dance in the rain."

Unknown

Please do not feed the fears.

Energy Vortex Mandala

Chakras are energy vortexes.
Mandalas are energy vortexes as well.

Chakra Mandala Meditation

Work with the Energy Vortex mandala or select another mandala to work with. Once you are seated, rest a moment in the beautiful space you have created. Close your eyes. Close your mouth and breathe through your nose. Count ten slow breaths and let your mind become still and your body relaxed. Gaze at your mandala with slightly defocused eyes, continuing to breathe as above. Take everything in while looking deeply into the mandala. Then let parts of it attract you with certain images, patterns, and colors. As you sit in meditation, the mandala will "speak to you" in a language your logical mind does not understand. Do not try to "answer," just let any thoughts triggered by the mandala come and go as you gaze. With eyes focused normally, begin a mental journey through the mandala, starting at the edge and moving inward. Take your time, noticing as much as you can, but once you have seen something, let it go and move on to the quiet of your center.

Your chakras are the energy vortexes that keep you healthy and vital. They connect you to your guides, intuition, and to the whispers of the universe. The chakras colors live within us. It is by stepping into our sacred center that we balance the spinning wheels of our life. The mandalas are activated, enlivened and personalized by your intentions. Yes, it is possible for a photograph, a painting a two dimensional image to have high frequency vibrations, that can interact with you and shift and change with you as you move through your life. With this in mind, focus intently on the mandala's center. As you gaze at the symbols, see the love and respect they have for one another and the relationship of their union with the whole painting. Energetically embrace positive reactions and feelings you might be having and let them find a home within you.

As you journey more deeply into the mandala, you will reach a door of light, a safe portal, that you can enter to connect with your own whirling, spinning, energetic self. Through the colors of the seven chakras and the images and symbols painted into the mandala, and your intention, you open yourself to the powerful and completely natural healing potential of your higher self. Close your eyes and enter with gratitude. In this beautiful silence, your inner wisdom and guidance will reveal to you what you can do for a more harmonious relationship with each of your energy centers. The more harmonious a relationship you have with yourself, the more harmonious your relationship will be with others.

With eyes open, take one more journey through the mandala, remembering in your mind's eye the messages and positive feelings that you have experienced. Symbolically return the mandala to its home, the sacred power center in your heart. Your center is where spirit crosses matter. It is where all is possible.

Close your eyes one more time and let the colors brilliantly swirl and whirl into the center of your mind's eye, which is symbolic of the center of your soul. As the colors become more and more energized and brilliant, they will vibrate into a shimmering, glittering, luminous, white light. Allow this white light to fill you, starting with your heart center and then slowly allow the white light to fill your entire body. Imagine your body encapsulated in this divine light. Visualize yourself glowing, beyond your physical body in the white light that is made up of all color.

This energy will stay with you for the rest of the day and beyond. When you are ready, open your eyes; bring your hands together in a little bow of joy and gratitude.

Right after a meditation, is a good time to make a note of any significant thoughts and guidance you may have received during the meditation.

Flower of Life Mandala

From the center of your magic circle,
You are one with your inner wisdom.
You are one with nature and with all living things.
To love yourself is to love and honor all.
It's that simple. It's that difficult. Once again paradox.

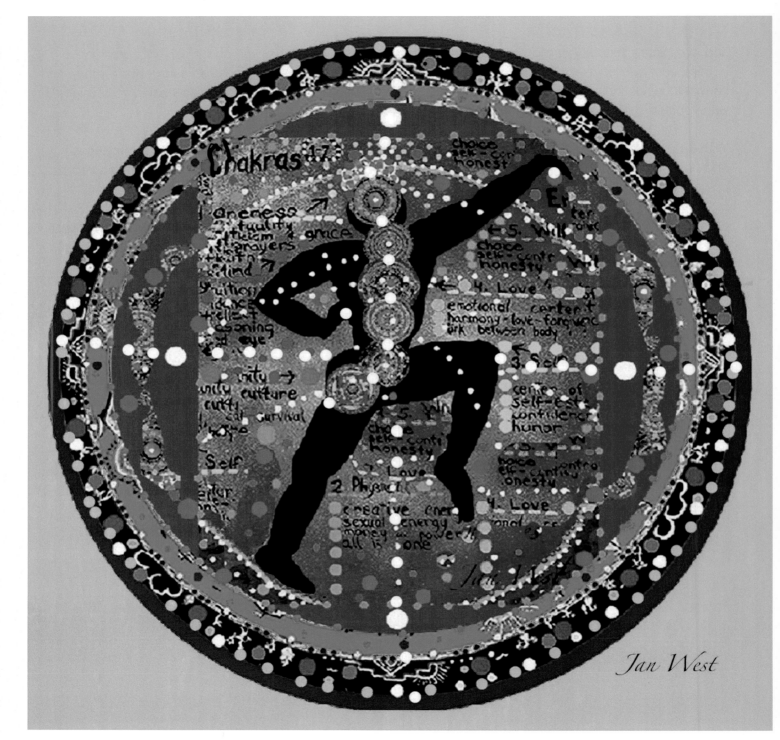

Circle Squared

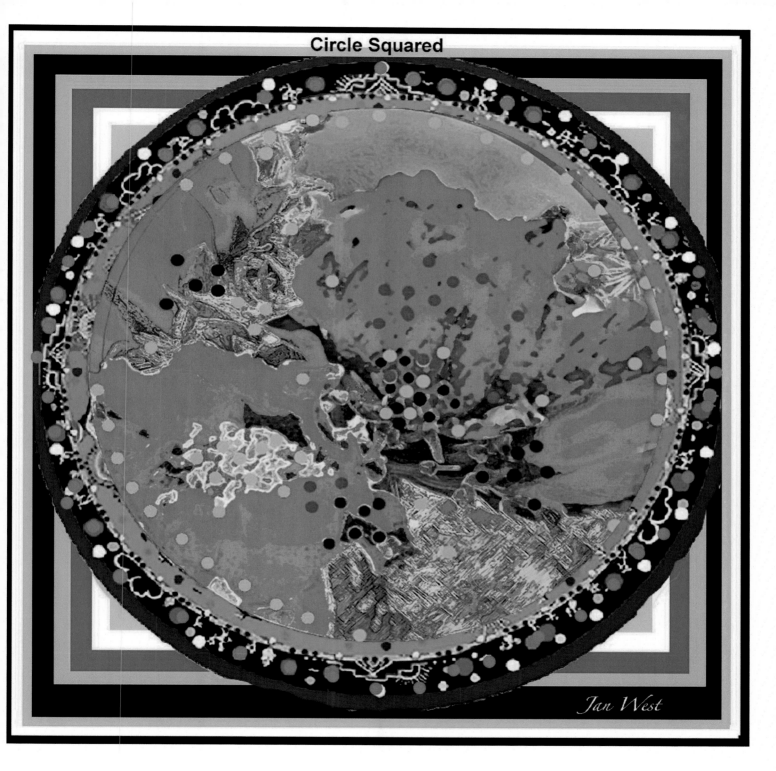

Jan West

Infinite Peace Mandala

The Citizens of the Earth Are One.

This mandala offers blessings for balance and peace on earth. The circle of houses is symbolic of neighborly love. As we learn how to love our brothers and sisters, so to, we learn how to love ourselves.

Eventually we will all belong to a world community, that is not divided by boundaries of land or thought. Hoping for such unity is radical, but essential, thinking. We are living within a fragile and closed eco system. What happens to one on Mother Earth, happens to all. Hopefully we can find our way to world peace without crisis. Care for each other, as well as the water, air and land that we share to survive, starts at home. Global healing begins here and now.

What we think, we attract to ourselves and create in our lives. Relax, breathe, smile, laugh often, and open yourself to the transformative powers of love. Allow the sacred seeds of peace to grow in your heart and to bloom in your mind and body.

The Infinite Peace Mandala creates a safe space for you to simply be.

We are one.

Jan West

Sacred Spaces Mandala

Work with the Sacred Spaces Mandala as a focus for your meditation or as a gateway into a pure and loving sanctuary, that will protect and guide you toward your highest potential. You cannot fail. Have faith and trust yourself and trust the Divine Mystery.

Our ability to honor beauty is a part of the reverence of life.

There are many sacred places both in nature and in man-made creations. Think of where you feel the most powerful and happy. Visualize this place whenever you need to become centered or as a gateway into stillness.

The ultimate sacred space is internal. It is where Spirit Crosses Matter. It is your Sacred Center.

"Your sacred space is where you find yourself again and again."

Joseph Campbell

Jan West

Jaguar Woman Mandala

Whatever befalls the earth,

Befalls the sons and daughters of the earth.

We did not weave the web of life;

We are merely a strand in it.

Whatever we do to the web,

We do to ourselves …

Chief Seattle

Mayan Mystics Mandala

A journey of a thousand miles begins with a single step.

Lao-Tzu

inner space

noun   *1* The region between the earth and outer space. The region below the surface.
The center of stillness.
2 The realm of the collective consciousness and awe.
3 The place where Spirit Crosses Matter.

outer space

noun   *1* The physical universe beyond the earth's atmosphere.
2 The Universe beyond conscious awareness made up of energy and consciousness.
3 The realm of the mystics, artists and innovators.

infinite space

noun   *1* The invisible consciousness realms.
2 The realm of the collective consciousness and the gods.
3 Nirvana, Source, Paradise Found, Bliss, Great Mystery

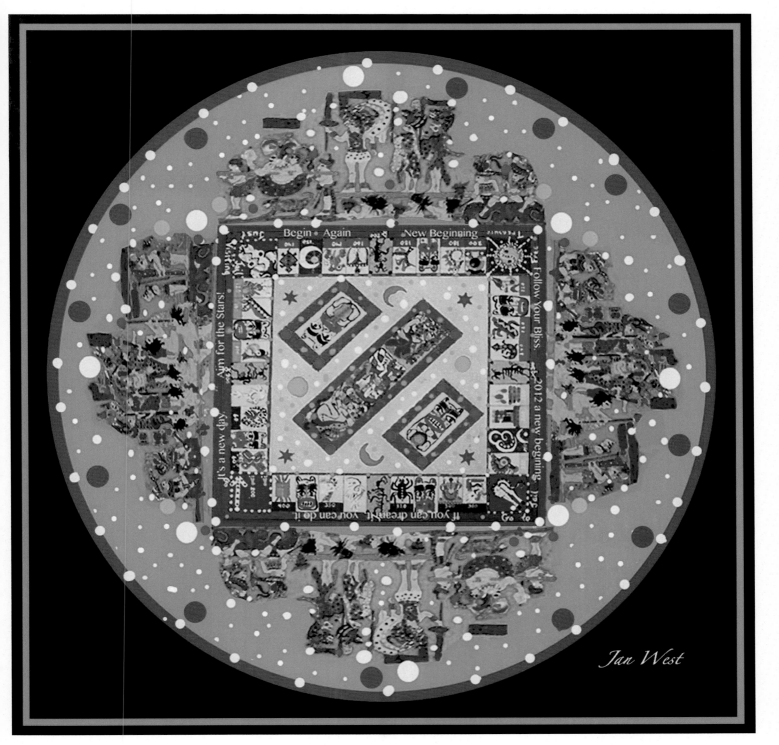

Fertility and Abundance Mandala

Fertility, prosperity, and abundance are incredibly healing energies. They are your birthright, to have, to experience and to share with others. Abundance is a state of mind.

Shift out of your "mind" and into the infinite possibilities of the present moment. It is a state of being, made up of Spirit, thought and emotions and a connection to all of life.

When you take action from your center, you can naturally attract and create prosperity in all areas of your life.

This mandala is designed specifically to help you consciously generate the resonance of abundance in your mind and heart, which is the first step toward transforming your physical reality. Use this mandala to attract greater levels of abundance and prosperity and joy in your life!

Jan West

Igniting Passion Mandala

Mandalas touch us at conscious and unconscious levels.

Let the flames of the mandala burn away your fears and negativity. Work with this mandala to release all that is not working for you in your life. Embrace your strength, power, courage, and creativity absolutely.

Allow yourself to be mighty.

This is a time of new beginnings and accomplishment. Now is the time to take honest inventory. Decide what you want, love, use, and need. Keep that. Feed that. Continue on course if it feels correct. Alter course if and whenever necessary. Look closely at what no longer serves you. Look at what needs releasing. When you release something physically and energetically, you allow it/them, to continue on, as well. Live and let live. Take stock, make the necessary adjustments and begin again.

By creating a void, we are saying yes to the new. We are allowing room for possibility to bloom and grow. The very act of releasing and opening, shifts your frequencies, vibrations, magnetism and a whole lot of other great stuff. Lighten your load and focus on what you care about most. There is no time like the present and no promise of tomorrow. Move forward with courage, integrity and discipline. Trust that you are supported by a force that is both benevolent and eternal.

The phoenix always rises.

Trust the process.

Trust yourself as you move forward with courage and determination.

Jan West

Big Changes Mandala

A Single Spark Ignites A Mighty Flame

A channeled intention, utilizes the power of our physical and mental bodies to join us with our eternal body. A fully integrated self, is then empowered to transmit intentions/prayers, out into the cosmos.

Launched prayers, serve as scout, transmitter, receptor, and architect. They are supersonic carrier doves, that align our intentions with the frequencies of the universe.

Intentions create a mystical pathway that is a power packed portal, that propels us towards our best destiny. Luminous fibers; bands of high frequency magnetism, are created. They anchor us to and ceaselessly guide us towards, illumination.

The marriage of intention with mystery, unites us with our cosmic triad; *Inner* Space, *Outer Space and Infinite Space.* It activates our relationship with the Source of all power. We are changed by the experience. We are stronger, more balanced, and prepared to meet life's challenges and blessings.

This is a practical example of how the metaphor of stepping into the heart of a mandala, can be used to help us in our daily lives. We can learn how to use a tool, in this case a mandala, as a launch pad for our intuitive connection with the mind of the source.

We have everything we need for bliss here on earth. Opening, listening, receiving and properly doing, are the challenges of the human condition. By stepping into our center and by moving out of the analytical and the intellectual realm, we open ourselves to probability. Our relationship with our *Trinity* goes beyond time and space. It is the basis of all that is good.

When we let go, and say YES to it all, we become a ready vessel.

" The release of atomic power has changed everything except our way thinking. "

Albert Einstein

Jan West

Egyptian Mystery School Mandala

Creativity and Inspiration

When you delve deeper into yourself, into Mystery, into solitude, beyond the ego, there is a resonance of Spirit, a motivation of soul, called inspiration! Inspiration fosters pure creativity and exhilaration on all levels of your being. When inspiration is present, motivation is heightened and it moves us into action.

This mandala of inspiration can easily help lift you out of states of procrastination, confusion, frustration and fear. It reveals the knowledge of days gone by. Secret teachings, ancient wisdom, alchemical symbology and practices, are painted into the stories on this time defying disc. Symbols and imagery, are able to connect with the viewer beyond two dimensional limitations.

Use your imagination, let go of preconceived notions, outdated thinking, control and of course fear. Let go and experience the lightness of time beyond time and mind beyond mind. Sit in your center, in stillness and allow yourself to wonder.

Focus upon your goals and dreams, and connect with a more positive self, who is filled with joy, freedom, and fulfillment. Inspiration raises our vibrations and attracts prosperity of all kinds. Inspired thinking, is a beacon leading us towards the proper manifestation of our highest aspirations.

Commit Absolutely To Your Chosen Path.

Jan West

Slice of Life Mandala

"We had no churches,

No religious organizations,

No Sabbath day,

No holidays,

And yet,

We worshiped."

Chief Geronimo

Jan West

Light, More Light Mandala

What Comes Next?

Music is to time, what architecture is to space.

In life, as in music we are always asking ourselves, "what comes next?" In both music and architecture we can never see or hear the whole at once. We are always anticipating.

One may think that a mandala can be seen in a single glance. Not so. Every mandala has a secret entryway built into it, that leads the willing initiate inward. The view from the pinnacle is a rich landscape, filled with hills and valleys. It is an ever changing diorama that is related directly to the passages of our lives.

The mandala provides a portal into the diorama that goes beyond time and space. It connects us, when invited, to Source.

When we emerge, we bring with us everything we need to move forward towards our highest destiny.

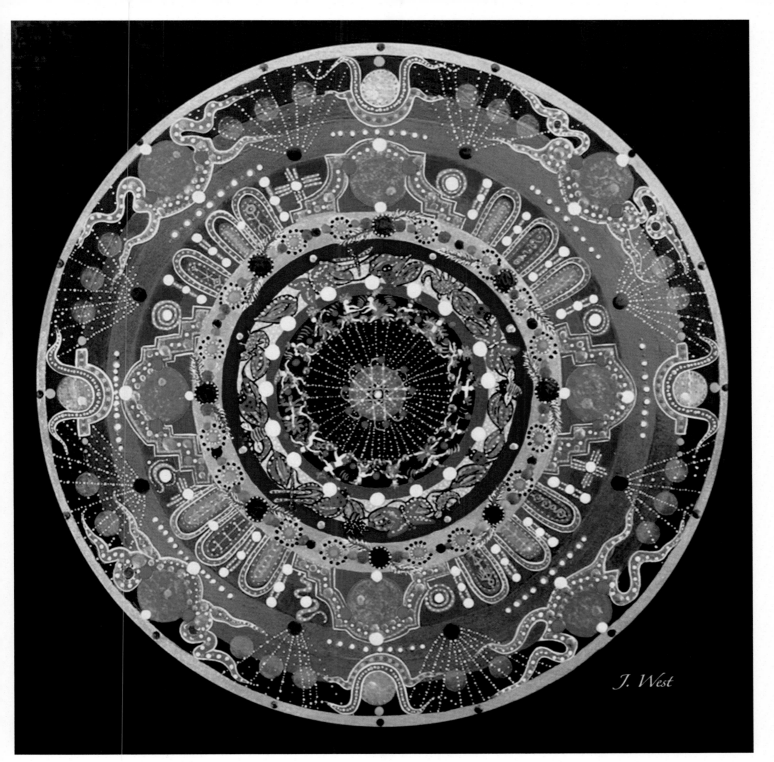

Orbs are Mandalas.
They are sacred circles, that are filled with stories of the ages.
They are filled with messages and energy. Like the chakras Orbs and Mandalas
are energy retention vortexes that can be invited to help us along in our evolution.

There are two ways to live. You can live as if nothing is a miracle;
or you can live as if everything is a miracle.   ~ Albert Einstein

Go to the truth beyond the mind.

Doves of Peace Mandala

Allow the doves of peace into your heart. Hold the vision of outer and inner peace. As above, so it is below. As it is in the world, so it is within our hearts and souls.

The Peace Mandala will serve as a direct portal in to your Sacred Center of hope, trust, and wholeness. Allow yourself to feel the self-esteem, dignity and the strong light of your true essence. Allow the Mystery to manifest within your being.

Each morning, we begin again.

We are all beacons of light.

Follow joy. Follow love.

Follow the Light.

Jan West

She Who Knows Mandala

Barn's burned down.

Now I can see the moon.

Masahide

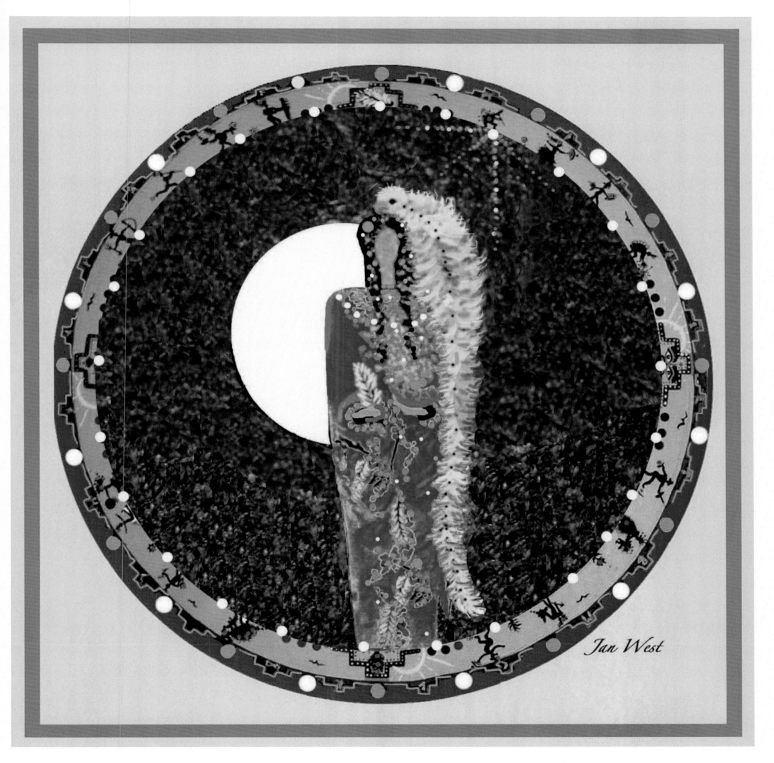

Jan West

Four Directions Medicine Wheel

Where Spirit Crosses Matter

The Medicine Wheel is a symbol that incorporates the four directions. Its spokes point north, south, east, and west. The four quarters are traditionally colored red (west), yellow (east), black (south), and white (north) representing the races of man, the seasons, and the stages of life from childhood to old age. The circle represents the earth, the moon, and the planets. It is symbolic of the circle of life and all creation.

The simplicity of the symbol is profound. It represents the many aspects of the four directions. We humans experience the four directions all the time. We see forward, but not back, and when we are facing forward, we have two sides. The four directions are a part of our biology and our psychology. The cross is represented in the medicine wheel.

For me it symbolizes, where spirit crosses matter. I visualize a small circle around the center of the cross, representing, Source, the center of all. Wholeness. Divinity. Balance. All are represented symbolically in the medicine wheel. They are archetypes of the highest order. As such, they are powerful carriers of symbolic meaning.

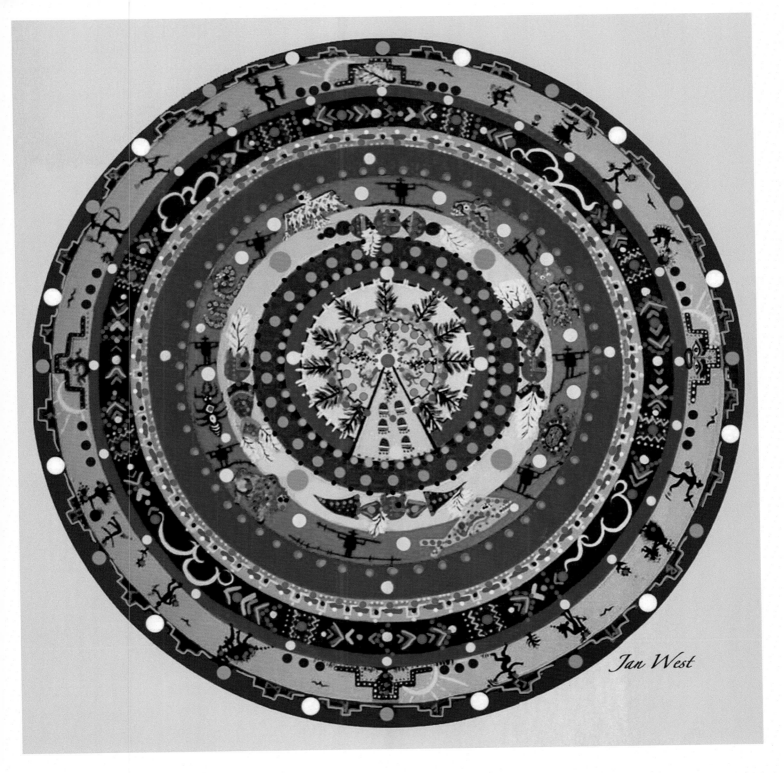

Jan West

Bridge over Troubled Water Mandala

We build too many walls and not enough bridges.

Isaac Newton

Jan West

The Sphinx Knows Mandala

Mysteries of the Ancients

Legend has it, that a secret chamber or room is carved into the limestone, under the left paw of the Great Sphinx. The legend is that this secret chamber is the great "Hall of Records" of the lost continent of Atlantis. The "Hall Of Records" is thought by some mystics and new agers to house the Akashic Records.

The Akashic Records are believed to contain all knowledge and all wisdom ever accumulated throughout time. They are understood to have existed since the beginning of creation and even before. The Records refer to the matrix of consciousness that created reality. One could look upon it as a library of light wherein one can access all information.

Whether or not this secret room exists, is irrelevant to me. Proving the existence of a collective consciousness, an actual library of luminosity of 'all knowing', is equally unimportant to me.

What is important is to think about these ideas symbolically. We know that we are made up of energy and consciousness. We also have examples in our daily lives of things functioning invisibly. We can all think of times when our thoughts have affected our reality.

My suggestion is that we step outside the box that so clearly defines physical reality, into the realm of the mystics and sages. I invite us all to step into the realm of the Great Sphinx.

Use this mandala as a portal into the Library of Light. The 'Hall of Akashic Records" is accessible to you, if you so choose. Spend some time there and you may be surprised by how real it becomes.

Every step of the journey, is the journey.

Jan West

Red Rock Mandala

This mandala is surrounded by the timeless red rocks of Abiquiu.

From the solitude and wisdom of the natural world.

We become one with all that is and all that ever will be.

In nature, we become connected with the natural cycles of life.

Nature is our truest connection to the Great Mystery.

As we care for Mother Earth, so we care for ourselves.

There are many pathways into Mystery.

The natural world is made up of Vortexes and Gateways into Source.

Access if you dare!

The choice is yours.

Jan's Medicine Wheel Mandala

Abiquiu, New Mexico

Sacred Space

"You have noticed that everything an Indian does is in a circle, and that is because the Power of the World always works in circles and everything tries to be round.

In the old days, all our power came to us from the sacred hoop of the nation and so long as the hoop was unbroken the people flourished. The flowering tree was the living center of the hoop, and the circle of the four quarters nourished it. The east gave peace and light, the south gave warmth, the west gave rain and the north with its cold and mighty wind gave strength and endurance. This knowledge came to us from the outer world with our religion.

Everything the power of the world does is done in a circle. The sky is round and I have heard that the earth is round like a ball and so are all the stars. The wind, in its greatest power, whirls. Birds make their nests in circles, for theirs is the same religion as ours. The sun comes forth and goes down again in a circle. The moon does the same and both are round. Even the seasons form a great circle in their changing and always come back again to where they were.

The life of a man is a circle from childhood to childhood, and so it is in everything where power moves. Our teepees were round like the nests of birds, and these were always set in a circle, the nation's hoop, a nest of many nests, where the Great Spirit meant for us to hatch our children."

Black Elk, Holy Man of the Oglala Sioux 1863-1950

Nuts and Bolts and Volts Mandala

To the disdain of my mentor, I call this mandala, *Nuts and Bolts and Volts.*
It symbolically and energetically projects recordings of knowledge. This mandala is a user's manual for science, engineering, construction, learning, and thinking. Imagine it to be an intergalactic micro-chip. A cosmic transmitter to which you are the receiver.

Consider your own body being made mostly of space. Close your eyes and experience the space that you're made of and the space around you vibrating like a tuning fork. Visualize ripples in a pond radiating outward after a stone is thrown into the water. Imagine that your rate of vibration is equivalent, to the information pouring in and out of you, in the same way that a radio is tuned to a certain frequency. Tuning allows you to hear a specific radio station clearly. In the body, if the brain is the receiver, then the tuning dial, is the heart, which defines the frequency of information received, and which can be altered by your emotional state.

The electric energy which motivates us is not within our bodies at all. It is a part of the universal supply, which flows through us from the universal source, with an intensity set by our desires and our will."

~Walter Russell

"Only those who attempt the absurd will achieve the impossible."

~M. C. Escher

Jan West

No Time Like the Present Mandala.

Be right here, right now. Call to action.

Brains, bravery, courage and action are required now. Starting is always the hardest part. Start locally. Start with the people and places that you touch in your daily life. Start somewhere. Do something. Do the next best thing that causes no harm. Your efforts will grow exponentially and touch more than you will know. Change and transformation are guaranteed when your wheels are set in motion.

The era we are now living in, is a tipping point. We are participating, literally and figuratively, in a challenge for survival. We are experiencing the devastating effects of a long standing abuse of the planet and each other, in scary and mythological ways. A kryptonite infused snowball is barreling down on us, with stunning velocity. Danger. Danger. Wake up. Danger. The snowball needs to be corrected, redirected, dispersed, stopped, repurposed and hopefully annihilated, immediately. I mean, yesterday. Replace the disastrous projection with progress and illumination.

Radical change, ingenious minds, invention and bold, cooperative action, is required to save ourselves. We need compassionate and brilliant leaders to help us tip the scale towards our best and brightest possibilities. What could be more important? What could be more thrilling than to save the planet and to make it a better place for all to live on, now and for the future. We can do it, together, I know we can. How about you? Are you in? On your mark, get set…GO!

Our senses enable us to perceive only a minute portion of the outside world.

~ Nikola Tesla

Wonder is the beginning of wisdom.

~ Socrates

The history of science shows us that theories are perishable.

With every new truth that is revealed we get a better understanding

of Nature and our conceptions and views are modified.

~ Nikola Tesla

Go to the Truth Beyond the Mind Mandala

In a world where words cannot be trusted, where truth, sanity,
and reason are lost to so many, ART is a requirement.
During these Orwellian times, symbols are more important than ever.
Learning to read and interpret symbolic language is empowering.
It lowers one's chances of being led astray by dangerous puppet masters.

Reflections From Outer Space

*Suddenly, from behind the rim of the moon, in long, slow-motion moments, of
immense majesty, there emerges a sparkling blue and white jewel,
a light, delicate, sky-blue sphere, laced with slowly swirling veils of white,
rising gradually like a small pearl in a thick sea of black mystery.*

*It takes more than a moment to fully realize this is Earth ... home.
My view of our planet was a glimpse of divinity*

- Edgar Mitchell

Reflections From Inner Space

*The secret to change is to spend all of your energy
not to fight the old, but on building the new.*

~ Socrates

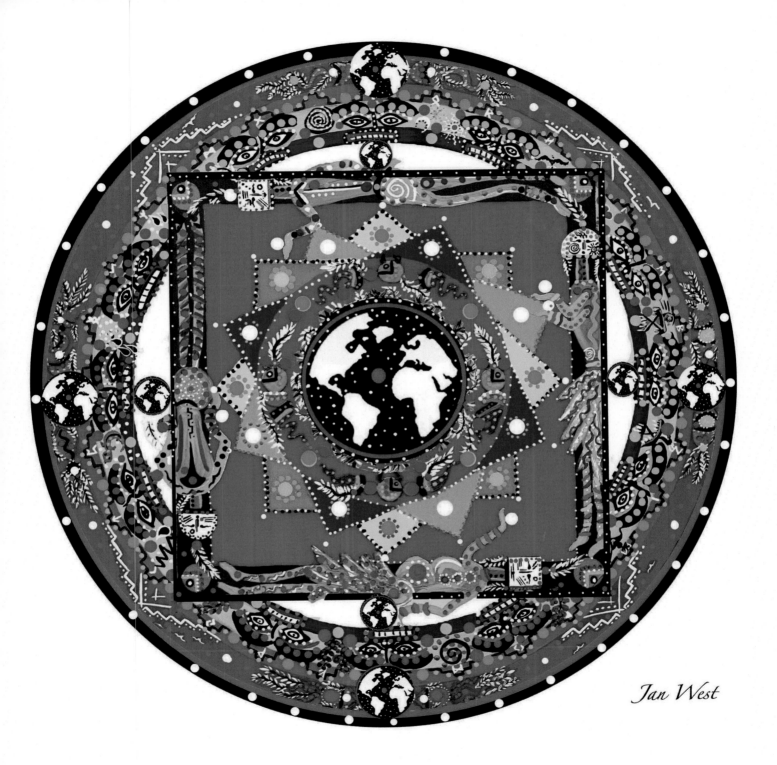

Jan West

Force

The Force is an energy field created by all living things.
It surrounds us. It penetrates us. It binds the Galaxy together.
The Force moves from within.
It has to do with the powers of life, as they are either fulfilled or broken
and suppressed by the actions of men.

~ Ben Kenobi to Luke Skywalker, Star Wars, by George Lucas

The prophets speak of a time when the tribes
of the Earth will come together as one.
They say, that when the clans join hands
in a circle of unity, the Earth will be healed.

Thank you for your time and interest.
I wish you the very best.

May The Force Be With You.
Begin again.

Jan

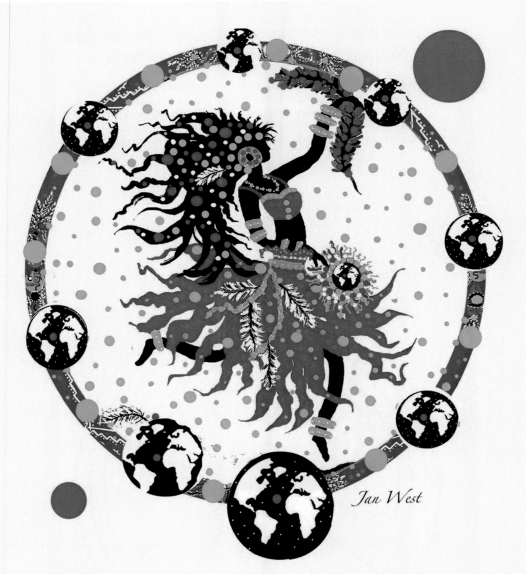

Jan West

The privilege of a lifetime is being who you are.

Joseph Campbell

Mandala Manifestation Worksheet

Write in the Prayer Wheel what you want to manifest in your life.
Visualize yourself and your life, as if it were already so.
Ask that your question, or prayer, be fulfilled swiftly and properly,
with harm to no one. Ask that your course of action, be clearly
mapped out in your mind's eye, so that you know what to do next.

So be it.

As a form of meditation, Ask a yes or no question.
Use your pendulum, over the prayer wheel and
open yourself to the answer.

Seal your prayer in a circle of white light
and place this piece of paper in a special place or carry it
with you. End your session with a prayer of gratitude and love.

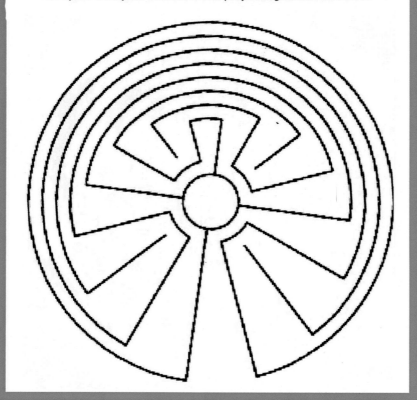

Mandala Worksheet: Release to the Universe

Write in the Prayer Wheel what you want to eliminate from your life.
Formulate clearly in your mind fears, habits, negative thinking, and all
that you want to release from your life, the world, your reality.
Visualize yourself and your life, as if it were already so. Ask that your
question, or prayer, be fulfilled swiftly and properly, with harm to
no one. Ask that your course of action, be clearly mapped out in your
mind's eye, so that you know what to do next.

So be it.

As a form of meditation, Ask a yes or no question.
Use your pendulum, over the prayer wheel and
open yourself to the answer.

Seal your prayer in a circle of white light
and place this piece of paper in a special place or carry it
with you. End your session with a prayer of gratitude and love.

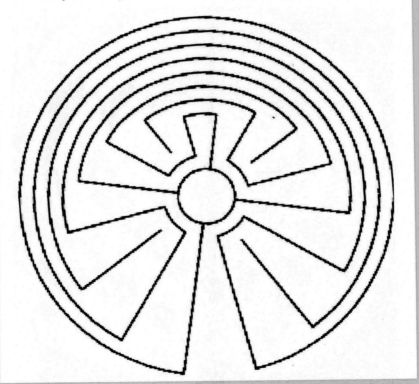

NOTES

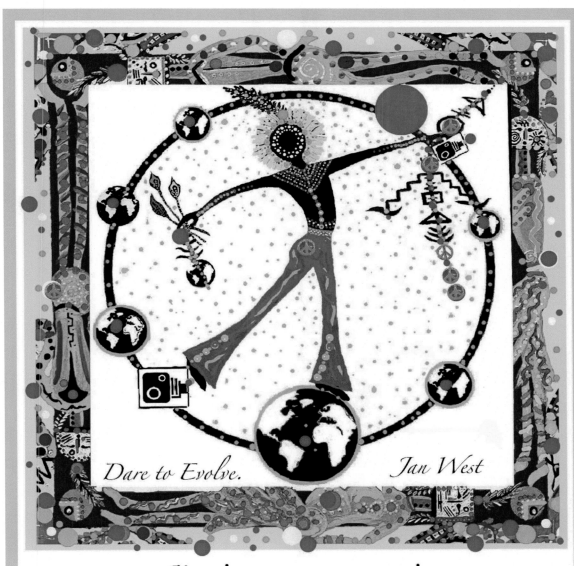

Dare to Evolve. *Jan West*

Circles never end.
Begin again.

About the author

Jan West is a painter and professional photographer. She uses paint and photography to explore archetypal, spiritual, and mystical themes.

She encourages all to embrace their personal power. Her message is that we are all interconnected beings of consciousness and energy and that our thoughts matter. Jan hopes her art supports and encourages the viewer's journey.

Jan believes the following:

Symbolic art, which is metaphor, is not to be taken literally. Any literal interpretation will always be so much smaller than its inspiration. When we assign a symbol to a thought, wish or prayer, it becomes an energetic, high-frequency transmitter, that is always shifting and growing. It becomes your own personal, ever-evolving healing tool.

Trust your journey. Step often and silently into the center of your sacred circle. It is there that you will find your truth.

Dear Reader.

Thank you for your time and interest. If you do find value in my work, I would very much appreciate your sharing it with others. I need your help to give my work wings. Thank you.

From my center to yours,

Jan

Buy Art!

All art presented in this book is available for sale:

Original paintings, murals, mandalas, and photography and commissions.

Archival quality prints and canvas reproductions; any size.

Greeting cards, calendars, meditation DVD's, book and more...

Commissioned Mandalas:

Jan will work with you to create your own mandala. The mandala that you create with Jan will be filled with your own personal symbols, stories, intentions, and energy. The process of creating your mandala with Jan is interactive and fun!

Please visit Jan's website and virtual Art Gallery at: www.JanWestArt.com
E-mail: JanWestArt@mac.com

Printed in the United States
by Baker & Taylor Publisher Services